INTRODUCTION

The city of Salisbury in south Wiltshire is famous for its Cathedral. Its lofty spire, the tallest in England, draws pilgrims and visitors from far and wide. They come to experience the Gothic masterpiece and also to view one of the original copies of Magna Carta displayed in its Chapter House.

The original settlement at Old Sarum, or Old Salisbury, is located two miles away, but when the decision was made by Bishop Richard Poore to move the Cathedral in the early thirteenth century to the gravel plain where the rivers Nadder and Avon meet, it became necessary for a whole new city to be built around it, and this was known as New Salisbury.

Although still small by city standards, it is perfectly formed. Planned from the start, it was laid out li

CW00816157

production of textiles. Salisbury's merchants became wealthy and, by the fifteenth century, the city was one of the largest in England.

Today, it feels more like a town than a city. There are no high-rise buildings and much of the medieval charm remains.

It is a lively and interesting place to visit with a good selection of independent shops nestled into its historic buildings, and twice weekly markets continue to this day.

Salisbury Cathedral at Dawn

© David Noton Photography/Alamy Stock Photo

OLD SARUM

Salisbury's origins lie at Old Sarum, a vast earthen Iron Age hillfort two miles north of today's city. Now greened with turf, in its day the steep chalk flanks would have glared white across the plains. Old Sarum is just one of a number of Celtic hillforts in the area but it is not precisely known who built them.

Records begin with the arrival of the Romans in 43AD. They immediately appreciated its position above a major junction of ancient tracks. They garrisoned the fort and used its elevation as a sighting line for at least five main roads, three of which converge outside the east gate. The middle of these is known as the Portway and connected London with Dorchester.

Old Sarum's glory days came with the Norman invasion of 1066. The existing power structures of church and state were radically redrawn to fit the new order and Old Sarum was chosen to be the administrative centre of a vast diocese that stretched as far as Dorset and Berkshire. The wooden castle was rebuilt in stone, a palace added and a Cathedral started. In 1086, Old Sarum was used as a magnificent stage for William the Conqueror to take delivery of the Domesday Book and accept the fealty of all England's landowners.

The Cathedral was consecrated in 1092 and became a centre of learning. One of the original copies of Magna Carta was kept here and a

liturgy 'Sarum Use' was established that would underpin religious practice for centuries to follow. But as a settlement, the site was impractical. Accommodation was limited with no room to expand. In winter, it was so windswept that worshippers complained that the howling winds drowned out what was being said.

Water was also a problem. The supply was restricted to one well that had to be shared between the military and the clergy. This often caused friction between them and in 1217, after leaving Old Sarum to go in procession to a nearby village, the clergy were humiliated to find the soldiers had deliberately locked them out of the city forcing them to spend the night outside.

Bishop Richard Poore sought

Bishop Richard Poore

Papal permission to move the Cathedral. It is said the new site was chosen by shooting an arrow from Old Sarum but the location that resulted was two miles to the south. It is more likely that this was a tale to cover the fact that the new city would be built on land owned by the Bishop rather than at Wilton. Old Sarum was abandoned without ceremony.

Although only part of the castle remains and the cathedral reduced to just its footings, the massive earthworks give the site a mighty presence. The outer bailey is free to enter, while there is a charge for visitors to the inner bailey and the castle ruins.

'Old Sarum' Watercolour by Constable 1834

Old Sarum was the original settlement before it was decided to move to lower ground.

3

THE CATHEDRAL

From the minute the first stones were laid, on the Feast of St Vitalis in 1220, an army of carpenters and masons set to work. Within five years, three chapels were completed, and by 1258 the Cathedral was consecrated by Bishop Giles de Bridport in the presence of King Henry III.

Having a new site allowed a complete design in one style without having to adapt to any previous building. Fresh ideas of geometry and aesthetics were laid out on a virgin green-field site and Salisbury Cathedral is now celebrated as a prime example of Early English Gothic architecture.

The design is usually credited to Elias of Dereham, who had just finished building St Thomas Becket's shrine in Canterbury Cathedral and who had also worked locally at

The Cathedral was completed in just thirty-eight years.

Winchester Castle and Clarendon Palace.

The builders certainly had to make quite a leap of faith when they started to dig the foundations. Four feet down they met a bed of gravel laid down by the river and they decided to build the Cathedral on it. It turned out to be a good decision that showed a considerable knowledge of engineering.

Should the gravel ever dry out however, the Cathedral's stability could be threatened. There is a place in the middle of the Cathedral where the groundwater level can be tested with a short measuring stick. This isn't only to check for rising water as many

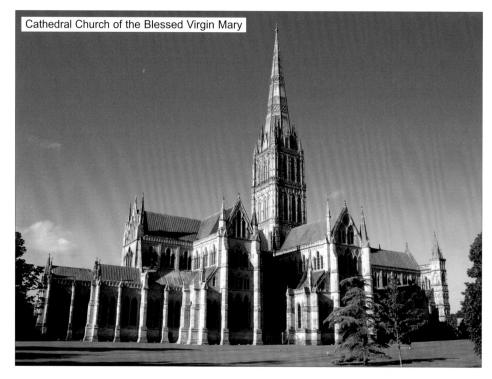
Cathedral Church of the Blessed Virgin Mary

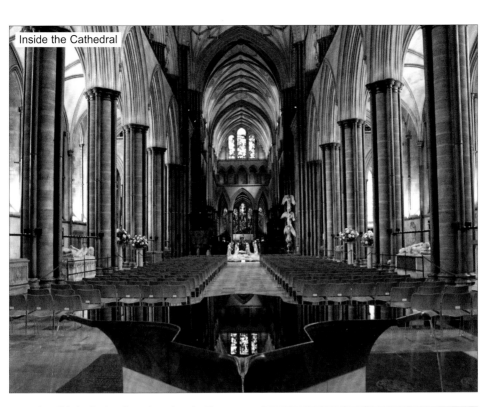
Inside the Cathedral

people think but also to check the gravel bed is not too dry.

These unusually shallow foundations are supporting a considerable weight. Part of the Cathedral's beauty is that it is created out of just two types of stone, all of which had to be quarried and brought overland to the site. The bulk of the stonework is in a fine-grained limestone from near Tisbury, known as Chilmark Stone, 18 miles west of Salisbury. This is a beautiful and durable material that weathers in the open air to a warm green-grey tint, staying creamy and fresh indoors.

The towering, slender pillars are of a contrasting dark limestone, known as Purbeck marble, from the coast 45 miles to the south. Though it is actually limestone, not marble, it certainly justifies the name, as it can be polished to a gleaming, almost

The glass for the windows would cover three acres if laid out on the ground.

black shade. In all, 60,000 tons of Chilmark stone and 10,000 tons of Purbeck stone were needed.

When it was built, Salisbury Cathedral had 365 windows, neatly equating to days of the year. What is less well known is that it also contains 8,760 pillars of Purbeck marble. Although no records exist, it's surely no coincidence that equates to the hours in a year. Credit for the construction is also given to the master mason, Nicholas of Ely. Under his direction, the masons, backed up by carpenters, would have found in Salisbury Cathedral a lifetime of work stretching ahead of them.

THE SPIRE

The Spire was not in the original design of the Cathedral and was not added until around a hundred years later.

With the medieval church at the height of its powers, spires had become very much the fashion. Salisbury Cathedral didn't need one to hold a bell, there was already a free-standing bell tower with a ring of ten, and it wasn't designed to have one, but the church authorities swept aside such practical difficulties and Salisbury had a spire soaring 123 metres (404 ft) into the air.

The higher levels were built from inside, from timber scaffolding which

The spire leans 70 cm to the south and 45 cm to the west.

can still be seen. Wooden ladders reach up to fifteen metres (49 ft) below the capstone where there is a north-facing 'weather door'. To go further, it is necessary to go outside and climb. An old plumber called Halley did so in 1665 and used the capstone as a barbeque, roasting 'a shoulder of mutton and a couple of fowls upon the top'.

Above the original lantern stage is approximately 6,500 tonnes of added stonework. This has worried almost everyone who has set foot in the Cathedral ever since. The Purbeck marble pillars of the central transept bow alarmingly under the considerable weight even though bracing arches were added.

Sir Christopher Wren famously surveyed the spire and found it to lean 27½ inches (70 cm) to the south and 17½ inches (45 cm) to the west. The spot is marked on the floor of the central transept and shows just how

Engraving of the Cathedral & Bell Tower

6

Wooden scaffolding inside the spire

far it is leaning off centre. Most of Wren's suggestions were carried out over the next fifty years, and no further leaning has been detected.

At the time of building, Salisbury's spire wasn't the highest in England, or even in Wiltshire. Malmesbury, Lincoln and the original St Paul's Cathedral were all taller. But all these have now collapsed. Salisbury Cathedral's spire, that doubles the height of the building and adds impressively to its appearance, has for several centuries been the tallest one in England.

Its lofty height has often attracted lightning; first in 1431, and again in 1641. A further strike in 1741 caused a serious fire. A lightning conductor

Before the 19th century, people would climb to the top of the spire to show off.

was fitted at the beginning of the nineteenth century and at the time was the longest lightning conductor system in the world.

An interesting way to see the spire is to take the tower tour. Lasting approximately ninety minutes, it lets you see the structure of the Cathedral not normally on show. The ascent, including 332 steps, takes you up to the base of the spire where you can go outside and enjoy a view of the city from above.

Bowed Pillars

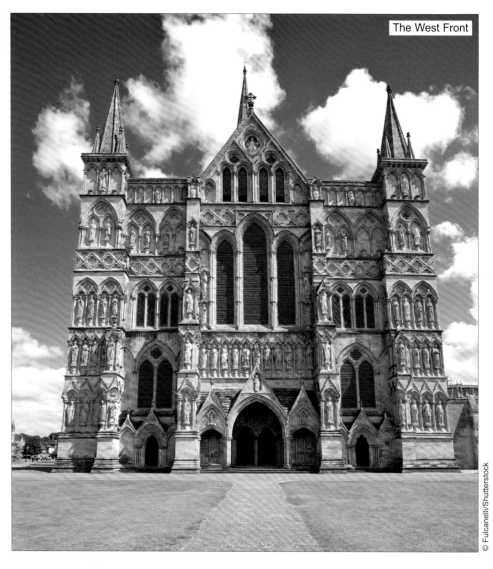

© Fulcanelli/Shutterstock

THE WEST FRONT

The West Front is a screen wall, designed to impress, and is wider than the combined width of the nave and aisles. At the top is a striking central gable that marks the end of the nave and two stone spirelets on either side. Three central windows flood the nave with light, while smaller windows on either side illuminate the aisles.

The most striking elements of the façade are the serried ranks of niches packed with individual sculptures. There is a clear structure to the various tiers. The lowest tier is designed to honour local worthies, above them are displayed doctors, martyrs and virgins, apostles are next, Old Testament figures and prophets feature even higher and to top them all is a tier of angels.

The niches are mostly populated with sculptures, with only the top two levels showing gaps. There are a few spaces amongst the tier of prophets and a drastic thinning out of the top level, the angels. What is most interesting, perhaps, is that for most of the Cathedral's life the niches were almost all empty. Even though they seem to provide a natural home to individual works in stone, they remained unoccupied until the nineteenth-century. A detailed drawing of the West Front in 1820 certainly shows only the buttress niches containing sculptures. The ones visible today came as a consequence of G. G. Scott's restoration in 1870. Immediately below the main triple west window is a row, covering nine quatrefoil openings, that certainly dates back no further than Victorian times.

Their lack of antiquity doesn't take

There are sixty-seven statues on the West Front of the Cathedral.

away from their power. Each figure is beautifully carved with individual expressions and exists as independent works of art in its own right.

At ground level, the West Front has three entrances, each with triple gables and finials that drop to grotesque waterspout heads, roofed with weathered stone. The central triple gable is larger, and has a statue of the Virgin Mary with a lily above the centre arch. This arch opens to a suitably impressive doorway that can do justice to major religious ceremonies and processions; although generally, all the doors on the western façade remain closed as visitors usually enter through the Cloisters.

West Front Detail

INSIDE THE CATHEDRAL

From outside, Salisbury Cathedral's size is concealed, to some extent, by its spacious surroundings. Inside, it stretches huge, light and airy, providing spacious settings for a number of significant memorials.

The Cathedral today differs from the original design due to a major and controversial refurbishment undertaken by James Wyatt between 1789 and 1792. Outdoors, he demolished the bell tower and levelled the graveyard. Inside, he removed the stone screen that sheltered the choir, cleared all the chantry chapels and rearranged various tombs. This opened up the vista inside the Cathedral, and was perhaps his most positive contribution. He also removed the remaining medieval grisaille glass from the windows and whitewashed over the medieval painting that once covered the ceiling.

One of the more unusual sights in the Cathedral is the original Cathedral clock. This is the oldest

> The columns supporting the spire are distorted from carrying the extra weight.

working mechanical clock in the world, still powered by a pulley turning rope-bound barrels in a wrought iron frame. Constructed in 1386, it doesn't even have a face; these hadn't been invented and its only role was to ring the bell, on the hour every hour. Before this, the community would have had to rely on sundials, with their 'temporal hours' flashing by in winter and lingering through the summer days. Only astronomers divided hours evenly all year, and this clock's effect on daily life would have been revolutionary.

Other highlights include a huge thirteenth-century cope chest for storing ecclesiastical robes without folding them, an impressive organ, and the 106 timber stalls of the quire. At one point, the interior was filled with chantries, funded by local

The Tomb of William Longespée. Half brother of King John, his was the first burial in the new Cathedral in 1226. Centuries later, a poisoned rat was found in his skull which suggests he had been murdered.

The Mompesson Tomb

dignitaries to provide privately funded afterlife prayers to ease their passage to Heaven. Wyatt's reforming zeal swept all of these away and only the Audley Chapel remains. It is worth a closer look for its fine stonework and painted, vaulted ceiling.

Wyatt also rearranged the tombs, leaving the Mompesson tomb facing the wrong way round, with feet pointing away from the altar. Of the medieval tombs, the most impressive is that of Bishop Giles de Bridport, with finely carved openings and narrative scenes illustrating periods of his life. A more modern memorial is a revolving etched prism dedicated to the artist Rex Whistler who died in the Second World War. It is hauntingly beautiful and deeply affecting because it was made by his brother, Sir Laurence Whistler CBE, who survived. One of the most interesting views is upwards in the Spire Cross, in the middle of the Cathedral. The curve of the marble columns as they strain under the weight of the spire is impressive and unsettling.

At 17.30 (16.30 on Sundays), the Cathedral comes to life with a choral evensong performed by the Salisbury Cathedral Choir.

Fourteenth Century Clock

The Cloisters

CLOISTERS & CHAPTER HOUSE

Spreading out from the Cathedral's south, the Cloisters are the largest in Britain. This is surprising because there was no monastic foundation attached to the Cathedral, and they would have only been used rarely for processions. Once, the upper stone arches were paned with grisaille glass. This has long gone and they are now open to the elements, scarred by iron bars added for structural reasons.

The Cloisters enclose a lawn that is shaded by two cedars of Lebanon. These were planted in 1837 to mark the accession of Queen Victoria and it's interesting to see how far they've grown.

The main use of the Cloisters is to provide sheltered access to the Chapter House, an elegant little structure that, despite its modest size,

is surely one of the greatest achievements of the thirteenth-century architects.

The Chapter House, closely modelled on the Royal Chapter House that had just been constructed at Westminster Abbey, is an octagonal building with a ring of soaring stained-glass windows, centred around a slender pillar. The design was very much a product of its age. At the time of its construction in the 1260s, English masons had just mastered the ability to build with elegant stone frameworks. Had it been built a hundred years earlier, it

The Cloisters were used as a prison in the seventeenth century.

would be a much darker building.

Instead of being a simple imitation of its Westminster model, Salisbury's Chapter House became a significant improvement. It has a much more elegant blind arcading in the lower wall and a superb medieval frieze above, telling all the important scenes of the first two books of the Bible: Genesis and Exodus. These images start with the Creation, and go through the full range of Old Testament stories. The building of Noah's Ark is there as is the destruction of Sodom and Gomorrah, and even the building of the Tower of Babel is squeezed into a frame. The carvings are bright and sharp, with considerable artistry.

Below this frieze, arches reach down to generously sized seats arranged around the outer wall. There are seven to a bay, trumping Westminster's five, so in all it could serve as a meeting place for fifty-one people. This used to be where the

Chapter House Seats

clergy would meet to discuss ecclesiastical affairs. It would have been quite easy to do as the room is designed to amplify sound. You can speak perfectly normally but still be heard in every part. Now it is the usual home of the Cathedral's copy of Magna Carta, the best preserved of the four originals to have survived through the centuries.

Fan vaulting inside the Chapter House

MAGNA CARTA

Magna Carta is one of the most famous documents in the world. It has come down through the ages as a symbol of justice, fairness, and human rights. For centuries, it has inspired and encouraged movements for freedom and constitutional government.

When it was issued by England's King John in June 1215, it was an attempt to prevent a civil war between the king and his powerful barons. The terms were agreed at Runnymede and comprise of more than sixty clauses covering many areas of the nation's life, including the right to a fair trial.

Elias of Dereham, key architect of Salisbury Cathedral, was involved in the negotiations and brought one of the original documents back to Old Sarum. When the Cathedral moved to Salisbury, Magna Carta came with it. Although the charter was updated and further copies made, only four of the originals still exist. One is kept at Lincoln Cathedral, and the British Library has two, but Salisbury's is by far the best preserved.

Magna Carta was written in Latin by hand on vellum, made from sheepskin. Vellum was made by soaking the skin of a lamb in mineral lime, then scraping it clean and stretching it to dry. Even though sheep were plentiful around Old Sarum, the process of making vellum was expensive and so skilled scribes had to keep their writing very small and fill every millimetre. The sixty-

The document is written on a piece of vellum measuring only 35^1/$_2$ cm by 18^1/$_2$ cm.

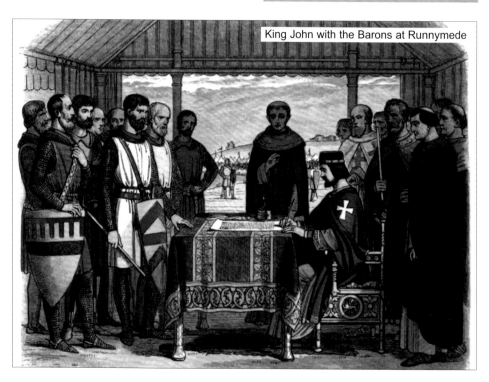
King John with the Barons at Runnymede

Salisbury's copy of Magna Carta

three clauses had to be packed onto one sheet. Vellum is exceptionally durable. Paper would never have survived for so long.

The ink used on it also has a fairly esoteric origin. It was made from oak gall, the lumps that are formed when wasps lay eggs in the leaf buds of an oak tree. These would be boiled with iron salts to produce ink. Pens were fashioned from the wing feathers of a goose or swan. Right-handed scribes would use quills from the birds' left wings. Medieval documents like this were not signed, but sealed, and at the bottom of Salisbury's Magna Carta you can see the marks where King John's seal was once attached.

By the 1400s, its influence was waning. This seminal document might have been lost had not the conduct of King Charles I, two hundred years later, focused attention back onto these laws that restricted royal power. Radical lawyers used Magna Carta to challenge the King in a growing dispute that was to escalate into the English Civil War and ultimately Charles' execution. For this reason, Magna Carta took on a renewed status as the cornerstone of English liberties. Even today, four of its clauses are still part of English law, including the fundamental right to justice and a fair trial.

King John's Seal

15

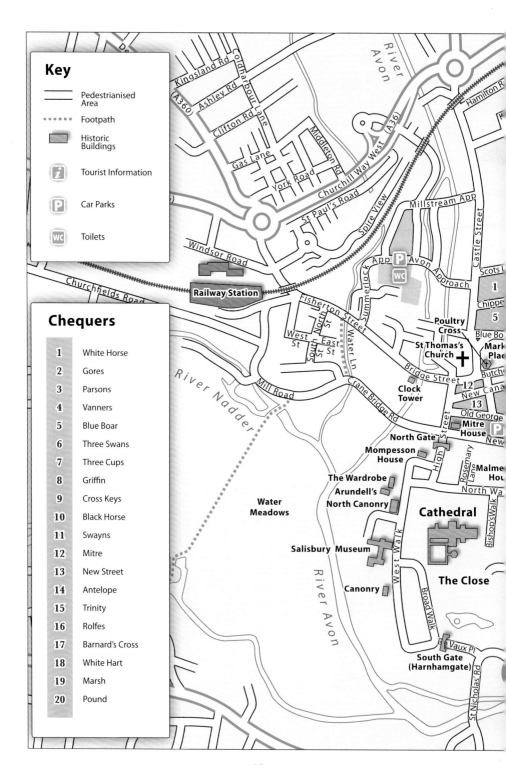

Key

- ——— Pedestrianised Area
- ······· Footpath
- Historic Buildings
- **i** Tourist Information
- **P** Car Parks
- **WC** Toilets

Chequers

1	White Horse
2	Gores
3	Parsons
4	Vanners
5	Blue Boar
6	Three Swans
7	Three Cups
8	Griffin
9	Cross Keys
10	Black Horse
11	Swayns
12	Mitre
13	New Street
14	Antelope
15	Trinity
16	Rolfes
17	Barnard's Cross
18	White Hart
19	Marsh
20	Pound

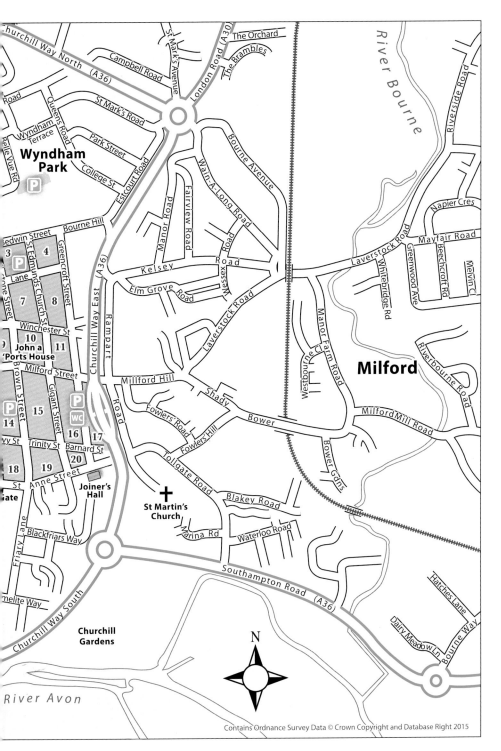

North Gate of the Close

THE CLOSE

Today, The Close provides a tranquil retreat away from the bustle of the city. This area around the Cathedral has a range of impressive buildings, many of them are Grade I listed, and arranged around manicured lawns. Measuring 80 acres, it is the largest Cathedral Close in Britain.

Laid out at the same time as the Cathedral, The Close was designed to provide homes for the clergy, who were expected to pay to erect suitable dwellings to suit their position. But several of the canons, already stretched by the cost of contributing to the Cathedral's construction, struggled to afford an appropriate ceremonial home and it later became accepted to allow the houses to be used by wealthy laity.

The Close was granted the right of sanctuary in 1317 and by 1327 this was formalised by an encircling wall. The wall was largely built from materials salvaged from Old Sarum and carved stones that were clearly from the old cathedral were used at random in the wall's construction.

The Close was once at the heart of a power structure that extended across the city and beyond. But the Bishop's power was limited in 1612 by a new charter that restricted his influence to only the area enclosed by the walls. The Bishop still had stocks and a gaol within but his jurisdiction no longer extended over the city's main prisons and pillories. When the gates were closed, The Close could be completely separated from the rest of the city. It even had its own private constables that patrolled the grounds,

The Close was under the jurisdiction of the Church.

18

keeping peace and order until 2010.

There are three public gates. The North Gate enters The Close from the High Street and holds a statue of Edward VII. This is one of a series of statues to occupy the niche: the first was of Henry III.

Giving access from the junction of St John and Exeter Streets, on the east side of The Close, is St Ann's Gate. The room above the gate was once a chapel; hence, the arched window, but in the eighteenth century the room was used for concerts and Handel is thought to have given his first English performance here. The South Gate or, as it is more often called Harnham Gate, is less ornate.

The Close Wall with salvaged stones from Old Sarum

In 1786, the tombstones around the Cathedral were removed or laid flat under the new manicured lawns.

It didn't need to be as when it was built it led out only to the river and the water meadows. Even now, these three gates are shut at night from 11pm to 6am.

St Ann's Gate

19

MUSEUMS

Salisbury Museum

Prime amongst the city's museums is the Salisbury Museum, where it would be easy to lose a few happy hours. This is housed in the King's House, once the property of the Prebendal of the Abbots of Sherborne, rebuilt in the fifteenth century and was for many years a teacher training college for ladies.

The museum came into existence when the drainage channels that once ran down many of the city centre streets were cleared to introduce underground sewers. So many relics from the medieval age were found, it became obvious there was a need for a museum to look after them. While these keys and cast-offs are still fascinating, there is plenty more to be seen here, including the Salisbury Giant with his Hob Nob and paintings by Turner, a drawing by Constable and works by Augustus John and Rex Whistler. A final highlight is the permanent Stonehenge exhibition, which adds a depth of understanding to the iconic stones without the crowds that jostle around the site itself. The remains of the Stonehenge Archer can be found here along with four carved chalk plaques from the area.

Just to the north of the Salisbury Museum is Arundells, home to Sir Edward Heath, former Prime Minister from 1970 to 1974. This mainly

'Salisbury from Old Sarum' by J. M. W. Turner, 1828-1829

Mompesson House

eighteenth-century property is set back from the main road in two acres of city centre garden. The interior is packed with a tasteful collection of sailing and musical memorabilia, ceramics, bronzes and more. The walls display an impressive art collection. Artists include Singer Sargent, Piper, Churchill, Sickert, Lowry, John Nash and Augustus John. Now run as a charitable trust, Arundells is open to the public through the summer months but closed in winter.

North again and 'The Wardrobe' is the museum of the Infantry Regiments of Berkshire and Wiltshire. There are major exhibitions devoted to both the World Wars but with rather more unexpected glimpses into history. The museum provides telling insights into countless lesser-known battles, including the American War of Independence, the China Wars, and the Peninsular War with Napoleon.

Around the corner on the northern side of The Close is one final museum, Mompesson House. The Mompesson family are now best-known for their garishly-painted tomb in the Cathedral although their family home has a more dignified appeal. It is a beautiful Queen Anne house that was used as a set for the 1995 film version of 'Sense and Sensibility'. The furnishing is all of the period apart from a fruit cake that is changed every few years. The house is also home to the National Trust's largest collection of glassware.

Five of Turner's original watercolours are housed in Salisbury Museum.

Map of The Chequers, 1773

THE CHEQUERS

The Chequers are a fine example of medieval town planning. At the same time as the new Cathedral was being built, a new city was laid out as a series of parallel streets running north to south and east to west. Bishop Poore owned the land and the plots were rented to tenants who built their houses on them. This grid system was inspired by ancient Roman cities and is similar to the American city blocks of today.

The Chequers in Salisbury are not entirely regular though, as the Bishop's revolutionary plan was to run water through the main streets from the Bishop's Mill on the River Avon. The streets, therefore, needed to follow the ground's natural contours. These canals were designed to keep the city clean and to carry rubbish away. They used to run down the centre of the roads, leading to the town becoming known, somewhat grandly, as 'The Venice of England'. But in 1737, they were confined into brick channels along the road-sides when they began to

cause a problem to the increasing traffic.

The city was deep in farming country with livestock markets every week so, in fact, through much of their life, Salisbury's waterways were little more than stinking open sewers. They were removed altogether a hundred years later after a series of cholera epidemics.

Over time, The Chequers were named after inns or the wealthy merchants who lived there. Hence, you have twenty chequers in the medieval town, including Three Swans, Antelope and Swayne's.

In the Victorian age, many British cities saw industry move in but despite its best efforts this never happened in Salisbury. Neither was it bombed in the Second World War, so most of The Chequers still follow the exact lines laid down by the original design.

To stroll around this historic area is a rare pleasure and there is plenty to catch a visitor's interest. Many of the original timber-framed buildings remain and others, equally old, are hiding behind modern façades. The

Chequers combine a real sense of history in a comprehensive range of shops, restaurants and bars. The major chains are here but most often confined within two of the three city centre malls. Salisbury trends to independent specialists, with arts and craft shops, boutiques and specialist food shops.

The city's ring road diverts much of the through traffic away from this part of the city giving it the warm, languid air of a typical Wiltshire market town.

'The High Street, Salisbury' by Louise Rayner, showing the water channels

HISTORIC BUILDINGS

Salisbury has a wealth of historic buildings. Many of them are medieval, and they stand alongside eighteenth and nineteenth-century properties.

The elegant timber-framed building on Queen Street, near the Guildhall, dates back to 1425 and was the home of the wealthy merchant John a'Port. Surprisingly, the adjoining building to the left, with the modern façade, is far older. It was built in 1306 and is thought to be the oldest still standing in Salisbury.

The city's very first house was built for Bishop Poore to live in while the Cathedral was constructed, and stood on the corner of New Street and High Street. The house that stands here now is known as Mitre House and is marked by a painted bishop's mitre on the wall. It is still customary for a newly appointed bishop to robe himself here before going to the Cathedral to be enthroned.

The Odeon Cinema on New Canal has a fake medieval façade that was added by Pugin in 1834. Step inside the lobby to find a genuine medieval hall with beautiful timber beams. This was once the house of John Halle, a rich wool merchant, MP and four times mayor of the city.

The substantial property occupying 3/5 Minster Street, next to the Haunch of Venison pub, is particularly interesting as its history is documented back to the late fifteenth century. This imposing four-storey property includes shops on the ground floor and was a typical city centre home to the wealthy. In contrast in Guilder Lane, a row of cottages survives, where the poorer citizens would have lived and worked.

Later, notable buildings include

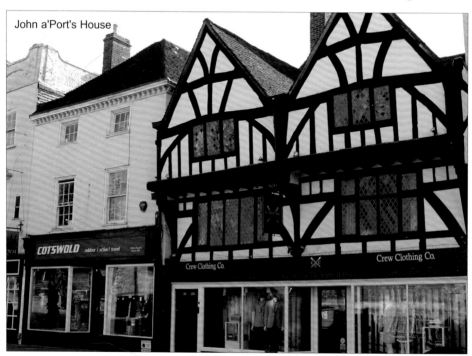

John a'Port's House

Humanoid carvings on Joiners' Hall

the Joiners' Hall on St Ann Street. This was built in the early seventeenth century at the time when Salisbury had a considerable reputation for woodworking. The blend of Elizabethan, Georgian and Victorian styles allow for plenty of fine woodwork to show off their craftsmen's skills. The humanoid carvings on the façade are worth a closer look. They seem to have recognisable male heads on top of grotesquely female bodies. It is thought that this was a veiled insult by the joiner, Humphrey Beckham, who had fallen out with some local individuals.

Just inside St Ann's Gate and viewed on Malmesbury House is a sundial that shows the date as well as the hour. Interestingly, it uses the old Julian calendar that was used in Britain until 1752. In the switch over to the Gregorian calendar, eleven days were lost.

The Clock Tower, also known as Little Ben, is a charming landmark on

Fisherton Street. This was built in 1892 by a Dr John Roberts as a memorial to his wife Arabella; it is on the site of the city's gaol and incorporates some of its stones in its base.

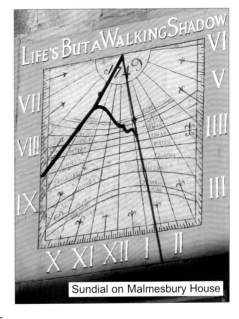
Sundial on Malmesbury House

25

The New Inn

HISTORIC PUBS & INNS

Pubs have always played a big part in Salisbury's life and many remain. The White Hart and the Red Lion are two of the largest hotels, with carriage yards that allow you to see inside the ancient chequers and imagine what went on behind the streets.

The Red Lion in Milford Street is one of the oldest hotels in England, with medieval parts dating back to 1226 when it was a hostel for stonemasons. It is known inter-nationally for its collection of clocks. Prisoners of war, captured from the Spanish Armada, carved the case of their Skeleton and Organ Clock.

Although the big hotels are more focused on accommodation than beer, traditional pubs are easy to find. The New Inn on New Street hasn't been new for many centuries and its half-timbered façade oozes character. Behind, it has a lovely secluded garden with a fine view of the Cathedral's spire.

In St John Street is The Kings Arms Hotel. This four-storey timber-framed inn is another of Salisbury's oldest inns although its major historical claim was in 1651 when royalist supporters planned King Charles II's escape to France here. It has many hiding places including a sliding panel that leads to a secret chamber in the attic.

To the south of the Cathedral on Harnham Road, is The Rose and Crown. Situated as it is on the bank of the river, the view from the garden is one that Constable famously painted after visiting Salisbury in the 1800s.

The Haunch of Venison in Minster Street started as a thirteenth-century hostel for craftsmen working

The Haunch of Venison

on the Cathedral, but went on to become a brothel. It is rumoured that a tunnel ran between it and the church of St Thomas's so that the clergy could visit discreetly.

It is said to be the smallest pub in Salisbury and also claims to be the most haunted. The pub is divided into a number of small rooms, with oak panelled walls, pewter bar tops and plenty of character. Somehow, it manages to squeeze a restaurant into its creaky top floor but one thing that won't be on the menu is the severed mummified hand in the former bread oven next to the fireplace. This was found with some eighteenth-century playing cards during a refurbishment and is said to have belonged to a whist player caught cheating.

A number of pubs have settled in the medieval shops that infilled onto the marketplace. The Ox Row Inn and the Market Inn can both be reached from Butcher Row or the Market Square, where they spill out tables in the summer and contribute to the city's almost continental atmosphere.

Ox Row Inn

MARKET PLACE

For the local residents, life centred around the market. First sanctioned by King John in 1219, it was formalised in a royal charter in 1227, specifying a market would be held every Tuesday and a ten-day fair would take place in August. But soon after, the nearby town of Wilton was complaining there was a market happening in Salisbury every day. A 1315 compromise settled that Salisbury's market should be held on Tuesday and Saturday; a tradition that has continued to the present day.

While at the heart of the medieval city, the market was highly regulated. Products were often weighed and sealed before they could be legitimately sold, and were restricted to particular areas.

Corn could be sold only in the northwest of Market Place, while cheese, milk and fruit vendors clustered by a Cheese Cross that stood at the end of Castle Street. There was also a Wool Cross in the marketplace, situated where the war memorial is today, and Barnewell's Cross, at the junction of St Barnard's Street and Culver Street, was where the cattle market was held.

Butchers plied their trade along Butcher Row and Ox Row. Poultry and vegetable sellers gathered around the Poultry Cross, the only market cross to survive.

Today's marketplace is barely half the size of the original. Over the ages, buildings have encroached. St Thomas's Church established a religious presence; the Bishop's Guildhall was built so the church

> **In medieval times, the Market Place was twice the size it is today.**

'The Poultry Cross' by Louise Rayner

Market Place

could process its tolls and fines; and the Shambles of Fish, Ox, Oatmeal and Butcher's rows developed into proper buildings. They can be distinguished from the planned houses of The Chequers in that they don't have gardens, merely shopfronts opening on either side.

Though it may lack the size of the medieval market, Salisbury's market still prospers in the present day. At its heart is a Farmers' Market, distinctively trading from blue and white stalls. Locally produced goods such as smoked trout, eggs, meats, sausages bacon, cheeses and fresh bread are always on sale. There are even local wines on offer.

Other stalls sell a huge variety of goods: oils and olives from Italy, carpets, jewellery, kitchenware, watches and purveyors of wooden furniture. Various traders compete to sell fruit and vegetables and the aroma of freshly ground coffee, hog roasts and freshly cut flowers pervades a colourful, noisy and bustling commercial environment.

Salisbury Market takes place every Tuesday and Saturday except the third Tuesday in October when the Charter Fair comes to the city. There is a smaller Farmers' Market that takes place every Wednesday at the Poultry Cross, while continental and vintage markets appear on an occasional basis throughout the year.

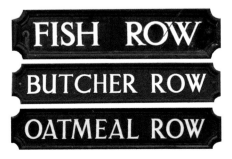

29

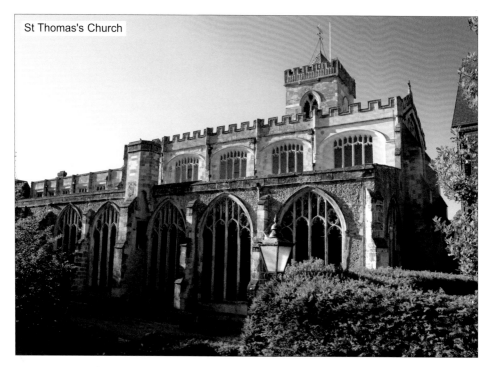

St Thomas's Church

CHURCHES

The oldest church in Salisbury, predating even the Cathedral, is St Martin's, whose foundations have been dated to 1100AD. The church itself is mainly from the fifteenth century, with a fourteenth-century spire and a thirteenth-century chancel. It was an important parish church for much of the city's development but is now somewhat cut off from the medieval chequers by the ring road.

No visitor to Salisbury should miss the church of St Thomas's, a notable encroachment onto the Market Square, probably first built out of wood in 1219 as a place of worship for the workmen building the Cathedral nearby. It was soon upgraded to stone and a bell tower added.

The church would once have been gloomy thanks to high box pews, but these have long gone and now the church is filled with light. Most striking is the superb medieval Doom Painting that fills the area about the chancel arch. God is in the middle, his disciples at his feet, with angels taking the fortunate to the Kingdom of Heaven while others, including bishops and crowned heads, are cast down to the Prince of Darkness.

These pictures showing the process of judgement after death were very common all over Europe though very few are left. St Thomas's is certainly the largest and best preserved in England.

We have the Puritans to thank for this. The doom picture was painted in

There are almost 250 carved angels in St Thomas's Church.

about 1475 and in the Reformation, the painting was obliterated by many coats of whitewash. It lay protected and forgotten for over 200 years until faint traces of colour were detected in 1819. It was uncovered and restored in 1881.

The Doom Painting isn't the only outstanding attraction of St Thomas's church. Look out for the eight paintings of angels in the chancel. These are Victorian, and their colour led the church choirboys to call them 'The Mustard Angels'. There are ten more, all left handed and playing medieval instruments, carved high in the chancel between the clerestory windows, and a hundred more angels, including one sticking out its tongue, on the fifteenth-century roof.

The organ is huge and this was originally given to Salisbury Cathedral by George III in 1792 and came to St Thomas's eighty years later as a hand-me-down.

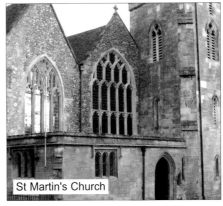

St Martin's Church

The last of St Thomas's secrets is in front of the tower's clock and is best seen from the Market Place, as it is hard to get a nearer view. There are two wooden figures in sixteenth-century armour, known as Jacks, who simulate hitting the quarter bells with a halberd. The installation dates back to 1581. It's not known how old the figures are but paint analysis suggests seventeenth century.

The Clock's Jacks

AROUND SALISBURY

Wilton House is a grand seventeenth-century mansion designed by Inigo Jones three and a half miles west of Salisbury. It is perhaps best known for its world-famous art collection but it also houses a selection of racing, classic and supercars, an adventure playground and twenty-two acres of grounds.

Time has been less kind to Clarendon Palace four miles to the east. In the Middle Ages, this was amongst the most lavish mansions in the country and attracted a stream of royals and aristocrats but it fell out of favour and was confiscated by Parliament at the execution of King Charles.

Three miles north of Salisbury, Old Sarum Airfield is the second oldest airstrip in Britain but has enjoyed something of a renaissance over recent years. Pleasure flights

Stonehenge is only nine and a half miles north of Salisbury.

can be taken in modern planes or a 1933 Tiger Moth. There is also a skydiving centre and the Boscombe Down Aviation Collection of vintage planes.

The most popular sight in the Salisbury area is Stonehenge, nine and a half miles to the north. This is the most architecturally sophisticated prehistoric stone circle in the world, precisely aligned to match the solar calendar. A new visitor centre does much to manage the flow of tourists but if the experience proves a little crowded a good alternative is the equally impressive megalithic complex at Avebury, 23 miles to the north. This is the world's largest prehistoric stone circle but is much less visited.

Stonehenge